The Cosmic Tour

poems by

Brian C. Miller

Finishing Line Press
Georgetown, Kentucky

The Cosmic Tour

Copyright © 2018 by Brian C. Miller
ISBN 978-1-63534-675-6 First Edition
All rights reserved under International and Pan-American Copyright Conventions. No part of this book may be reproduced in any manner whatsoever without written permission from the publisher, except in the case of brief quotations embodied in critical articles and reviews.

ACKNOWLEDGMENTS

I would like to thank the following magazines and journals for their publication of individual poems:

The Storyteller ~ "Just Write," Glass," "What I Saw Through The Lens."
Barbaric Yawp ~ "The Cosmic Tour."
The Shepheard ~ "Patience Of Faith."
Feelings of the Heart ~ "When Internet Dating Crashes," "View From My Treehouse."
Westward Quarterly ~ "Fluorescent Days."
Nebo ~ "Chemical Bond," "Passing Through."

I would like to thank my mom for her love and support, my professors at Penn State Altoona for inspiring me, Ann Bickel for the photograph, and Dawn Bawa for the beautiful artwork.

Publisher: Leah Maines
Editor: Christen Kincaid
Cover Art: Dawn Bawa
Author Photo: Ann Bickel
Cover Design: Ann Bickel

Printed in the USA on acid-free paper.
Order online: www.finishinglinepress.com
also available on amazon.com

Author inquiries and mail orders:
Finishing Line Press
P. O. Box 1626
Georgetown, Kentucky 40324
U. S. A.

Table of Contents

The Cosmic Tour 1
What I Saw Through the Lens 2
Glass 3
Daydreaming After Work 4
Passing Through 5
Chemical Bond 6
Laundry Detergent 7
Sitting on Leather 8
Just Write 9
Depth 10
When Internet Dating Crashes 11
Realism in a January Sky 12
Fortune Cookie 13
Patience of Faith 14
Listening to God 15
Fluorescent Days 16
College Life 17
The Wrinkled Paper 18
The Silent Song Screams 19
A Tanka for the Summer Solstice 20
Stranded 21
The Last Drop of Syrup 22
Runaway Balloons 23
View from My Treehouse 24
Looking Through Windows 25

*For all my friends who have supported me
throughout my writing journey....
(You know who you are)*

The Cosmic Tour

Side streets evoke traction in me
like the imprinting of ducks.
This neon rock got spray painted
when I was 9 years old.
It still sits along the side
of the road with faded cracks.
People said this street is me,
but girls will change me soon.
I just sighed and rolled my eyes.
In the midst of familiar streets,
and an hour talk outside my car,
I glance around her cheekbones.
The sight of her body outlasts blacktop.
I'm reading lines from the moon
and catching stars during a tour.

What I Saw Through the Lens

Years passed since I saw
the tilt of her head shining
her smile like a spotlight on me.
That smile traced around my shyness
and turned into my northern star.

I followed her star-lit eyes for two years
and felt the softness of her words
through clusters of college moments—
like our five hour talk on life,
and our view of Leo.

Tonight, I saw that northern star
through the tilt of this telescope.
I look high and even higher.
The higher you look in the sky,
the farther back in time you see.

Andromeda floats around the lens
as a dobro plays in a soft tempo,
backed by drums, like a soundtrack.
I'll always see that tilting smile
as long as the stars raise forever.

Glass

Other girls are like fireworks
that quickly fade to smoke
as we slowly get close.

But she can fill an empty glass
with shooting stars. Her eyes
can write on a piece of granite,

and write a number one song.
The melody soars through my veins
as she sips on a glass of 7-up.

She can also hold time
that makes me make up
on things I missed out on,

like brushing her braided hair,
and taking her hand in a neon world
full of youth and harmony.

Daydreaming After Work

Sometimes I wonder what it would be like
to have a wife. A woman who knows
I love music, coffee, and chocolate.
But hate elevators, airplanes, and bugs.
I wonder how it would feel to share
our finances, or share the sheets at night
the way seeds share dirt in a garden.

When the bathroom turns into a pond,
she gets mad because I'm not a plumber.
But we laugh at the silliness of the scene,
and the dirty word out of her mouth.
We could be a team in the kitchen.
I wash the dishes in dish liquid
while she dries and puts them away.

Passing Through

Fall breezes bite the leaves
off half-naked branches.
I shuffle through rusty leaves,
and my mind wonders to a time
when she locked me in a dream
that breathed life into me.
Other girls seemed to be like
a cloudy sky when the years aged.
She was an aurora igniting the sky—
A sight. I may never see again.

Chemical Bond

You are the woman who opened
up my universe. A unique inspiration
in the middle of a thunderstorm.
But sometimes words turn to regret
that hit me like stones on skin.
Instead of retaliating through anger,
you dusted off like a pro
and still held the candle
that keeps our friendship lit.

Laundry Detergent

We walked up and down aisles
at a crowded grocery store.

You studied the never-ending list
as my mind wondered through lights.

I started to think about the years
and chasing those girls in college.

You scanned down each aisle
for a bargain or a good laundry detergent.

It was then I noticed a strand of gray hair
hiding behind blond hair. Don't worry.

To me, that's like focusing on white
space in a book we wrote together.

Sitting On Leather

It always felt like I was walking
on neon clovers when she talked.
Maybe it was her verbal skills-
or the way she tilted her head
when I saw us through a mirror
in our own leather booth.
We blended like the beams
of a stretched-double rainbow
touching the ocean's waves.
She ignited a romantic side of me,
like taking her hand for a moment
and ignoring a nervous stomach
in our own leather booth.
If only I could rewind time,
we can continue the magic.

Just Write

A blank sheet of paper stares at me
and invisible stanzas move lines.

Your eyes lit up every time you saw me—
this image blinks around my poet's block.

The ink doesn't want to make a stroke
because you read my everything.

I hear myself say, "She's the pretty blond
wrapped around my beautiful life."

A blank sheet of paper stares at me.
I could feel the crease of your hand

holding mine, just enough to embrace.
Your unique mind created harmony

like your admiration of a peacock's wings.
But you flew away before I could catch you.

A blank sheet of paper stares at me.
I keep hearing, "Write a poem about me."

Depth

It's always cool to hear her laugh
linger from the receiver.
We keep topics saved in our files.

She talks about deadlines at the office
while she's managing to cook tacos.
I store that in my work and food files.

She's not a profile on a computer screen
because her blue eyes chased me to here.
I store that in my real files.

A silence never slips out of dialogue
as she talks about Jill's new dress.
I store that in my friends file.

A file of love even pops up
like a jack-in-a-box.
She wears bad luck badges too.

She sees my childhood through a window,
like playing tag in my backyard.
This depth causes our past files to max out.

Something interrupts our humor file,
which reminds me of a deeper reality.
Her daughter coos in the background.

When Internet Dating Crashes

Hope grew on this ground
like a palm tree in Denver.
But like an architect, he built
each message as high as the Taj Mahal.
He crafted his feelings in a box
she opened last week when they met
for the first time. But something happened.
A chandelier lights up the marble counter.
His phone, silent as an empty house.
A waterfall painting lurks in the corner.
The blue paint is smeared by a nearby cloud,
which reminds him how she has a piece of him.

Realism in a January Sky

A pile of snowflakes hovered my window.
Each crystal melted on heated glass
and disappeared, like my chances in love.
So I walked to a nearby snow field.
All I saw were a hundred snow steps
that I made without a compass. Each step
was like relationships gone astray.
In the middle of a snow squall,
one snowflake danced on my hand.
Gray and white crystals outshined the rest,
which reminds me of the special woman
God sent me. The moon spotted us
while we hugged tightly. The warmth
of her body erased years of solitude,
and snow filled up lost footsteps.

Fortune Cookie

I cracked open a fortune cookie
at a Chinese restaurant last week.
It stated: *Today you will be rich.*
I rolled my eyes—I'm far from rich.
But when I fumbled for a tip
in my blue pocket of dirt,
I found that phrase to be true.
I stared at the cross around my neck,
and the shine. I became rich in God
through golden memories He marked.
This is why I inherited rich blood
from a rich family line of wisdom
that is like a compass to a castle.
Here, I grew rich in knowledge
through every plate of life's lessons.
This is why I held the restaurant door
for my girlfriend before we entered.

Patience of Faith

> *Be thou removed, and be thou cast into the sea; and shall not doubt in his heart, but shall believe that those things which he saith shall come to pass: he shall have whatsoever he saith.*
> *Mark 12:23*

A heavy fog steamed up a rainbow
and caused me to write my goals
on clouds as the wind blew backward,
the boat forward. Reflecting on this goal
stirred up a prayer that seemed like yesterday.
I wanted my failures and fears to sail away,
and drown into the river that pulled me.
Immersing in faith became my main goal.

Six years have passed since that boat trip,
and my goals have not seen any light.
I walked to the pond with a bamboo cane
that made dent prints on even grass.
Fish constructed ripples of a cross.
I know Jesus listened to my goals
as he sat in the invisible lighthouse.

Listening to God

It's strange what the mind recalls—
the night before entering high school.
The rain filled up my nervous stomach
at 11pm, and I watched a chunk
of a branch crash in my neighbor's yard.
Wires on the rotted telephone pole
swayed to a song the wind just wrote.
I wondered if I would be accepted
as fear and excitement conflicted me.
Then a huge piece of thunder erased jitters.
Sometimes we worry and later realize
there was no reason to worry.
Now I know the storm show memory
was God's way of protecting me,
giving a story to tell my kids some day.

Fluorescent Days

A new decade marked my teenage mind
as a modal cannon stood in the school's hallway.
To me, it represented the mystery of time.
Chalkboards were replaced by white boards,
chalks were replaced by colorful markers,
and teachers taught from an overhead scroll.
Girls wrote notes in pink and purple pens
while boys wore Ultimate Warrior T-shirts.
I discovered the benefit of styling mousse,
but I kept quiet and reflected on this new life
as my friends traded and collected slap bracelets.
My trapper keeper always looked organized
with power writings on yellow-lined paper,
and blue pens tucked into the green net.

College Life

I remember lighting up my psychology book
while I annotated notes in the margins.
I leaped through articles of research
just to write a 12 page essay.

I remember walking around the pond
as the sunshine flashed through the trees.
Visitors fed the ducks after a study block
that always happened before economics class.

I remember memorizing scripts for theatre class.
Deadlines always made me start right away,
but I got stage freight on the day I got graded.
The time I put in translated to "keep trying."

I remember a trailer classroom that semester
in the dead of winter-no heat. Tough professor.
I scraped snow off my shoe and shivered
before analyzing a John Updike story.

I remember that pretty blond in Spanish class
leave as her body got smaller without a turn.
I wanted to say something to her as time raced.
She talked to a frat boy before I could catch her.

The Wrinkled Paper

I hold onto my pen and wish
that time didn't slip out.

The words I wrote twenty years ago
are a blurred form of a pen stroke,

but the meaning of the words are deep,
clear as yesterday's sunlight.

I walk and hear squeaks on the floor
and think about slanted lines on my face.

The Silent Song Screams

Quarter notes lay in his stomach
like a lost treasure in an attic.
He hears violins play in his head
with a rhythm of a tambourine.
All he does is tap and flap
to an unfamiliar beat.
His classmates think it's cool
when he tells them Woody Guthrie
wrote "This Land Is Your Land."
He stares at eighth notes
hiding in an open music book
while the class learns fractions.
Thoughts of a slightest hum
awaits his audience.
But silence slips out instead.

A Tanka for the Summer Solstice

Yellow jackets buzz
around a bed of pollen.
The sun greets summer
through a fresh coat of sun rays
that swallow the Earth's troubles.

Stranded

I'm stranded on this highway again.
Numbness fills my legs without direction.
My mouth-dry as sand. Exit signs lurk
through corners of foggy eyes.

I'm stranded on this highway again.
Pavement markings swirl around the road
and a string of acceleration lanes scream.
Debris blows around a chilly wind.

I'm stranded on this highway again.
Familiar couples walk toward me,
but run past me as hawks fly overhead.
I keep losing something, somewhere.

I'm stranded on this highway again.
My thumb is on the shoulder,
but blurry cars speed up the evening.
The boy in me finds serene memories.

The Last Drop of Syrup

I turn maple syrup
upside down
and watch
a slow drop
dribble
to the spout,
to the waffles.
It's ok to drown
in the wait
of the last drop
as the day
awaits me.

Runaway Balloons

Winds and rain pick up life
like a Tuesday hurricane.
Some days I'm a tornado
trying to keep up with life.
A flash flood of memories
explodes. Year 40 is on the radar.
I will settle for a framed mudslide.

View from My Treehouse

Childhood thoughts flashed
from the sight of my treehouse.
I could see the sunset lay
like a panoramic blanket.
Fear resisted each step
of the latter as I climbed.
I wrote in my journal,
listened to a Travis Tritt tape,
and daydreamed about girls.
Stars rotated with advice
as if to say growing old
is miles away without reach.
Memories are like rusted leaves
that blow and fall to the ground.
So I rake them with glowing eyes.

Looking Through Windows

When I lay on my bed
and slowly close my eyes,
each breath I breathe finds
those lazy summer feelings
of being a 12 year-old boy.
Shuffling through baseball cards,
cherry Hi-C on my lips,

and going to Church with my dad
on Sundays emerge. Hymns played
as I studied the gentle melodies.
I watched my dad pray and sign
by his bedroom window that night.
The lightning bugs on the screen
were as still as the summer air.

More summer thoughts pour each breath,
like seeing my dad by third base
after baseball practice. "Time to go."
Hymns continue to repeat in my brain
as I see my family at a food market.
My dad bought me a baseball sticker book
and a PB Max bar after practice.

Now I pray by the same window
with the same Church Hymns
bringing back a 12 year-old's feelings.
I know there is a window in Heaven
where my dad watches down on us.
It's stain glass full of memories
that live on like time on Earth.

Brian C. Miller was born in Altoona, PA in 1977. He received a BS degree in Elementary Education from Penn State Altoona in 2002. He worked for a year as a Special Education Aide and decided to return to Penn State Altoona. This time, he received a BA in English. It was here where he learned the craft of poetry. After graduating in 2005 from Penn State Altoona, he returned as a Special Education Aide for the Altoona Area School District.

He has won several poetry contests sponsored by the Blair County Arts Foundation. He volunteers for Arts Altoona, which is an organization that brings arts to the community.

In 2012, he had his first chapbook published by Finishing Line Press entitled, *The Blue and White Tent*. His poetry has appeared in *The Connecticut River Review*, *Barbaric Yawp*, and *The Old Red Kimono*.

He enjoys music, baseball, cooking, and spending time with his friends. He still resides in Altoona and can be reached on Facebook and at brianmiller34@netscape.com.

www.ingramcontent.com/pod-product-compliance
Lightning Source LLC
LaVergne TN
LVHW041517070426
835507LV00012B/1640